What Were They Thinking?

Avoid Behaviors and Attitudes That Can Ruin A Job Interview

Janice R. Jenkins

Published By: Janice R. Jenkins
janjenkinsmsed915@gmail.com
ISBN: 978-1-387-65787-2
Philadelphia, PA
Book Cover: Proebookdesigns

Printed in the United States of America

DEDICATION

Thank you Fred Scaglione

ACKNOWLEDGEMENTS

My family, The Youth Experience Success! (YES) Program at the Osborne Association in New York City, LeMaige Tapia, Sheila Mashack, Lanish Alston, Sylvia Fye, Angela Daidone, Ijeoma Baxter, Keith Hefner and Tom Brown of Youth Communication Inc., and the wonderful clients I have served over the years.

Many Thanks!

ABOUT THE AUTHOR

Janice R. Jenkins has held mid and senior level positions in the workforce development field since 2002. From 2012-2016, she led a mentoring project for young women professionals she founded. Janice was a blogger (under the name Janice Tosto) for the New York Nonprofit Press (NYNP) E-Newsletter (now New York Nonprofit Media) from 2009 to early 2015. Janice holds a master's degree in Guidance and Counseling from Hunter College of the City University of New York and earned a Professional Certificate in Career Planning and Development from New York University's School of Professional Studies. Janice is an aunt of two nieces and two nephews.

Contents

INTRODUCTION

In early 2015, a staff member from a New York City-based program serving youth with incarcerated parents contacted me and asked if I would give a work readiness workshop to her group. It had been a while since my last presentation to a youth group, but I readily agreed to speak.

My workshop topics included interview attire, essential or soft skills that contribute to success at work (for example getting to work on time, cooperating with co-workers, managing your time at work, fulfilling your job responsibilities, etc.) and the proper use of technology and social media in the job search. One of the things that energized me about speaking to this group was the opportunity to talk to the young people about avoiding some of the mistakes that job candidates made in some of my interviews.

I earned a graduate degree in Guidance and Counseling because my goal was to provide college and career counseling to high school students, especially those who came from low-income families like mine. But the job market was disappointing after graduation. It was difficult to find a high school counseling position. A viable option for me was to work as a career or vocational counselor in community based organizations and colleges where young people could be prepared for careers.

It was never my intention to have a position requiring me to hire employees. Serving as a career counselor and working directly with clients, preparing them for job interviews, was quite satisfying. But my supervisors noticed my leadership and management qualities, and encouraged me to pursue managerial roles and responsibilities, which required hiring staff.

No one really taught me how to interview job candidates. Taking notes from my own past job interviews, talking to seasoned professionals about how they conducted hiring interviews, researching interviewing techniques on reputable career information sites, and assisting colleagues with their interviews helped me develop my skills in interviewing job candidates.

It certainly felt strange to be on the interviewer's side of the desk as opposed to the job candidate's side. It was intimidating, but I was determined to become a skilled interviewer who selected the best candidate for a position. I wanted to be a personable and fair interviewer, because the anxiety that job seekers feel is not unfamiliar to me. Personally, every one of my own job interviews made me feel anxious! Most interviewers put me at ease, but some did not.

My practice is to be an interviewer who tries to make the experience as painless as possible. One of the most exciting things about interviewing is the potential to find a really great candidate who can help your team perform well. The moment when an interviewer realizes the right candidate may have emerged is exciting, especially if the interviewing process has been grueling.

The motivation for my writing this book is to remind job seekers that interview behaviors and attitudes matter! A Twitter post by Career Builder, a prominent online employment site, sums up the message of my book perfectly: "Your behavior, attitude and manners affect your chances of being hired."

What alarms me, as an interviewer, are the negative behaviors and attitudes presented sometimes by candidates in some of my interviews. In over 15 years of interviewing job seekers, I have met mostly good candidates. Even if they were not a fit for a position, they at least presented professionally. But I have also seen, with greater frequency, some good candidates jeopardize their opportunity to secure a position over some behavioral or attitudinal issue in an interview.

No interviewer will tolerate poor behavior or a bad attitude. The candidate simply will not get hired! As I am writing this, my eyes are fixed upon an August 2017 AM News(New York City) article from Reuters stating that one of the reasons employers were having a hard time finding workers was the negative attitudes of some candidates ("Job Openings At Record High, But Workers Don't Fit The Bill"). Increasingly, I have been seeing job announcements stating that the person hired must have a positive attitude.

It is especially important to me to share my experiences as an interviewer with new job seekers to help them avoid making the missteps some candidates made in their interviews. Some of the recent college graduates interviewed by me over the years had been found lacking in the preparation they needed to interview successfully. College students can benefit by taking advantage of college career services such as workshops and career counseling, as these are indispensable tools for adequate job preparation.

The sections of this book cover topics that have been addressed in my interview workshops, where the focus is primarily on how to prepare for interviews and how to conduct oneself in an interview. Appropriate interview behaviors and attitudes are emphasized.

Part One of this book offers some brief job seeking tips. This section is based upon a blog post written by me a few years ago. The qualities of a good job interview are covered. For those who struggle with talking about a professional weakness in an interview, suggestions are offered. Finally, job seekers are reminded to send interviewers a thank you note after every interview. There is an example of one of my thank you notes.

Part Two delves into the larger conversation about some negative behaviors and attitudes that job seekers will want to avoid in an interview. All of the anecdotes are about real job candidates interviewed by me. The names of the candidates have been changed. Some of these applicants might have been hired by me had their presentation been appropriate.

Part Three offers true accounts of some difficult interview experiences I had as a job seeker. My interviewers did not display the professional behaviors and attitudes expected of interviewers. This section emphasizes the fact that job seekers should remain professional in their behaviors and attitudes even when an interviewer does not. A humorous story is shared about the wrong way I chose to handle a dysfunctional interview.

Part Four features two anecdotes about candidates, Jeffrey and Esme, who were interviewed and hired by me. They interviewed well, but later revealed themselves to be poor employees. These incidents only demonstrated that the truth of who a person is always get revealed at some point. Display integrity in your interviews and on the job!

Part Five serves as a cautionary tale for those who have a difficult time with rejection. It is the true story of a man who was rejected for a seat in a training program after two interviews. After his rejection, this disgruntled candidate sent a barrage of inappropriate emails to my staff and me. Job seekers do not want to act in the manner in which this man did when faced with rejection.

In Part Six, you will read about my "feel-good" interviews. These include an account of one of my own interviews, where the outcome was my being offered a better job than the one for which I had originally applied. Also featured are two stories about my interviews with stellar candidates. One of these candidates was a woman hired by me who turned out to be such a phenomenal employee that she was promoted in under a year on the job! The other candidate was a personable young man who had been in the juvenile justice system and was seeking employment.

At the conclusion of the book, a brief list of some helpful career resources is offered. It is my hope that job seekers find this book helpful as they embark on their job search, prepare for job interviews, and map out their next (or first) career move.

A good job candidate is mindful of their behavior and attitude. Skills are important, but practicing good behaviors and having a good attitude are important too! Unfortunately, we are witnessing so much incivility in people's behaviors and conversations these days. But for an interviewer and employer, civility, good behavior, and positive attitudes never go out of style.

Thank you for reading!

PART ONE:
TIPS ON JOB SEEKING

"NS" (A FEW JOB SEEKING TIPS): The following is a blog post I wrote on job seeking tips for the New York Nonprofit Press E-Newsletter some years ago.

Before the Interview:

> Let potential references know that you are job seeking. I received a phone call from an employer regarding a reference for a person supervised by me years ago. We had not kept in touch, so getting the call caught me off guard. The professional thing for this person to have done was to send me an email or call me to give me a heads up, especially if we have not communicated in years. This person should have reached out to me and sent me a current resume. People do not want to feel used. One of my former employees is currently job seeking. She keeps in touch periodically, and always contacts me to let me know when to expect a call from a potential employer.

> Get a professional email address. Please don't send me a resume and cover letter with an address such as sexywhatever@wherever.com. Yes, this still happens.

Getting the Phone Call from an Employer to Set Up an Interview:

Emails are sent to candidates to set up interviews, but are always backed up with a phone call. When I call you, your message should be clear and brief. Employers don't have time to listen to music or silly messages. We just need to leave the message after the beep, and the beep needs to come as soon as possible.

The Interview:

Show up for the interview. (Yes, that's what I meant to write). Call or email if you cannot keep your appointment. When I write the letters "NS" on my calendar, that indicates that the person was a no-show, meaning they did not even bother to call me to cancel or reschedule the interview. Calling me after the fact does not suffice, unless there was an emergency that prevented the candidate from coming. That I certainly understand but do not understand people thinking that I have time to wait around. Someone else could have been scheduled in their time slot.

Make sure you bring copies of your resume with you to the interview. One of my colleagues in the workforce development field told me that some people actually catch an attitude when she asks for a copy of their resume at the time of the interview. They say "I emailed it to you." Please have a copy or two in case.

Watch What You Say:

Do not utter any expletives. A colleague told me that she recently interviewed someone who dropped an "f-bomb" during the interview. Glad I wasn't there. My jaw would have dropped and my eyes would have popped!

At a community partner meeting I attended at a Workforce 1 Center, an Account Manager who helps customers find employment talked to those of us in attendance about the difficulty she and her colleagues faced in finding suitable candidates for job placement. "We have a hard time finding good candidates," she said. The Account Manager went on to discuss some of the negative behaviors she and her colleagues often see in candidates (poor attitude, inappropriate dress and presentation). She said that candidates have to "be sharp and put their best foot forward." With regard to skills, she said that they were important, but added, "Your presentation and articulation will be considered."

At my agency's weekly case review meeting, one of the counselors publicly thanked Jonathan, the teacher on my staff, for the work he does with the clients. He thanked his colleague with his usual humility. When I was looking to hire a teacher, Jonathan's resume came across my desk. It was not like others I had received. It was not a poor resume at all, just different. Something told me to contact him. After my initial interview with him, Jonathan was asked to return to meet with my staff. They liked him as well. Three years later, we still like him. He does wonderful work. Employers like me will take a chance on someone like Jonathan when we see that there is a possibility to have a great worker in our organization, and I am sure that there are other employers who feel the same way.

I hope I have made suggestions that, if followed, will help make your job search fruitful.

WHAT MAKES FOR A GOOD JOB INTERVIEW?

Conducting job interviews can be exciting for me, but admittedly, interviewing can sometimes be frustrating and tiring. When hiring, no more than two or three interviews are scheduled for me in one day. Each job candidate is given serious consideration and my hiring decision is not made lightly. My interview notes are reviewed thoroughly and interviews are replayed mentally.

It is important for candidates to present well and have a good attitude. Candidates are expected to practice good hygiene and be neatly dressed. A smile, good eye contact, and a solid handshake are important because candidates get a nice smile, good eye contact, and a firm handshake from me. Candidates will even be offered a cup of water. A good candidate's phone is placed on silent because our conversation should not be interrupted. Good candidates do not answer phone calls during the interview and under no circumstances do they take a selfie during the interview! I recently attended a job development panel discussion and heard an employer state that he recently rejected a candidate for taking a selfie during an interview.

For me, the best interviews are those where the candidates have a conversation with me and take notes as we speak. Good candidates can tell me something about the organization (they have done some research), they display energy, enthusiasm, and offer good, descriptive examples of the work they have done. It is important for me to hear what they have accomplished at work, what they have liked about their work, and what they can contribute to my organization. I am always striving for good program outcomes, so candidates must tell me how they can help me continue doing good work on behalf of my clients. Candidates can also tell me about their use of soft skills in the workplace including punctuality, organizational skills, working cooperatively, making decisions, solving problems, and others.

Good candidates ask the interviewer questions. They inquire about the culture of the organization and about the person who will be supervising their work. These candidates find out if there are opportunities for professional development and learn about organizational challenges. There are so many questions candidates can ask an interviewer. Once a candidate asked me what I liked about my job. It was a wonderful question and I was all too happy to talk about my work and the great work the organization was involved in.

A good candidate will conclude the interview by asking about the next steps in the hiring process and will ask for my contact information.

The "A Few Helpful Resources" section of this book lists online career sites where job seekers can find sample interview questions. These sites will also have suggested questions that job seekers can ask of interviewers. Job seekers can also learn about illegal interview questions that cannot be asked on an interview.

IN WHAT PROFESSIONAL AREAS CAN YOU USE MORE DEVELOPMENT?

"In what professional areas can you use more development?" This is my so-called "trick" interview question, though it really is not tricky at all. Most times when this questions is asked by me, candidates respond "that's a good question." The candidate will think for a minute and most times, will stumble in their answer. Sometimes the question has to be rephrased.

When asking candidates about professional weaknesses, I do not use the word "weakness." My preference is to say "areas of development" because I want the candidate to reflect upon how they can grow their skills and improve their work. Is it that we get so used to talking about our strong points that we give no thought to areas where we need further professional development?

Interviewers who asked me about my professional areas needing further development were told about my desire to improve my computer skills. My level of computer proficiency is good but could be better. I have taken several computer classes over the years and am always open to learning more. Another area of development for me would be learning to manage my anxiety when giving presentations. My presentations usually go well, but in my nervousness, information sometimes get left out because of my eagerness to get through the presentation. I am now learning to meditate to help manage my presentation anxiety.

Recently, a man posted a hilarious story on Facebook about a candidate he had just interviewed for an internship. The man asked the candidate about his biggest weakness (his word). The candidate replied: "Seeing eye to eye with people who disagree with me." When asked about his biggest strength, the candidate stated: "Being right." Wow! Of course, he did not get the position.

For some candidates, it is their tech skills that need a boost. Some people may want to get better organized at work. Some would like to learn a second language to better serve diverse clients or customers. The answers are individualized, as long as the candidate's response is something connected to improving her or his performance in the workplace.

There are employers committed to their employees' professional development. They offer trainings to help their employees grow and thrive in the workplace. I always sent my staff to trainings offered within and outside of the organization or referred them to online training. The employees learned new skills and/or improved upon existing ones. And when my supervisors offered me the opportunity to attend trainings, I willingly signed up.

SEND A THANK YOU NOTE AFTER YOUR INTERVIEW

Career articles about post interview thank you notes often lament that many candidates do not send them. For example, a Monster.com career advice column referred to an Accountemps survey of HR managers that found only 24% of them received thank you notes after interviews. The column urged job seekers to send thank you notes as part of their job seeking process ("Should You Send a Thank -You Note After Your Interview?" by Monster Worldwide, Inc).

Candidates can send a thank you note via email or mail a typed or handwritten thank you note. Thank you notes should get out to the interviewer no later than 24 hours after the interview.

Thank you notes do not have to be lengthy. I have seen thank you notes ranging from five or six sentences to three paragraphs in length. In addition to writing a line thanking the interviewer, a candidate can briefly write about one or two highlights from the interview, and remind the interviewer why they are interested in the position and would be a good fit for it. Online career sites such as Monster, LinkedIn and CareerBuilder offer a wealth of information about writing thank you notes.

My practice is to send thank you notes after every interview in the job search process. My own thank you notes have been brief, averaging five to ten sentences. For example:

> *Dear Mr. Jones,*
>
> *Thank you for interviewing me for the position*
> *of Career Specialist for the LJ Johnson Career Program.*
> *I enjoyed learning about the position and speaking with you*
> *about research and workforce development. This position*
> *absolutely interests me!*
>
> *Thank you again for your consideration.*
>
> *Respectfully,*
> *Janice Jenkins*
> (Yes, the position was offered to me!)

Sending a thank you note does not guarantee that a job seeker will get a position, but it certainly raises their profile. In some cases, they may have been the only candidate, or one of a handful of candidates, to send a thank you note. Candidates, express your gratitude!

PART TWO:
WHAT WERE THEY THINKING?

The following anecdotes are examples of some of the interviews conducted by me over the years that ended unsuccessfully for the candidate. In each situation, some behavioral or attitudinal issue hurt the candidate's prospects of getting the job for which they had interviewed.

THIS IS THE FINAL INTERVIEW, RIGHT?

Never have I been hired at a company after only one interview. There were occasions where three interviews were the norm for me! Some people have told me about having to go through four or more interviews for a position. As a job seeker, I did not complain or question an organization's hiring process unless something seemed unfair. In that case, working for that organization would be of no interest to me anyway.

Eldon was a man interviewed by me for a position as an Outreach Coordinator. We had been having a difficult time filling this position and were anxious about this process and hiring the right person. Eldon did not have all of the qualifications for the position, but his resume interested me. He had some impressive experience in social media.

Eldon came to the interview on time and was dressed in a nice suit and tie. He was mannerly, and demonstrated great interest in the position. Eldon was told about the importance of the position to our program. He answered most questions well, but some of his responses were cliché and canned. Eldon kept saying "let me demonstrate that I am the best candidate for the job." He was invited back for a second interview with a couple of my colleagues and me.

During the second interview, Eldon had to make a presentation. His presentation was good, but a red flag was raised for me when Eldon kept asking me the same question repeatedly. He asked if he would get some time to get acclimated to his role should he be hired. I assured him he would. He made a statement about being "thrown into the job" that sounded off-putting to me.

My practice is not to hire people, "throw" them into a job and tell them good luck. New staff members are given a great deal of support from me to help them be successful in their new roles. Eldon seemed fixated on this idea of being "thrown into the job" and it concerned me. He was coming across as overly anxious. We ended the second interview by thanking him and telling him we would be in touch. Eldon was notified that some candidates would be invited back for a third interview.

My colleagues and I conferred about the candidates we had interviewed. They liked Eldon. My concerns about him were voiced but my colleagues felt he had been one of our better candidates! Sometimes interviewers do not agree. Eldon and another candidate were invited back for interviews with my supervisor. She was a tough interviewer and we would be very interested in her feedback.

The day before Eldon's third interview, I was meeting with my supervisor in her office when the Office Manager came in. She told my supervisor that she had confirmed the interview with Eldon, but was a bit put off by a comment he made. We looked at her and she told us that Eldon asked "This is the final interview, right?" At that point, I was really annoyed. VERY annoyed. To us, he was questioning our hiring process. We probably could have made a hire after the third interview, but what if our Executive Director wanted to interview candidates as well? Again, this had been a difficult position to fill and our ED wanted us to be successful with this important hire.

Eldon talked himself out of a possible job. This reminded me of when he was making his presentation during the second interview and repeatedly asked that annoying question about being "thrown into the job". This latest incident just validated my feelings about this candidate. My supervisor, who was also annoyed, cancelled Eldon's interview. An email message cancelling the interview was sent to Eldon. He did not have to worry about another interview with us ever again!

I'M NOT GOING TO WORK FOR PEANUTS!

Emily was interviewed by me for a Career Counselor position. She held a master's degree and had impressive work experience in the workforce development field. When Emily was contacted for the interview via email, she was given a job description and told the salary range. Emily confirmed her receipt of the email.

During the interview, Emily talked to me about how she would facilitate career readiness groups if she were hired. She rattled off the names of different career exploration materials and group exercises that she would use. Emily even taught me about some new career tools. We also talked at length about engaging and counseling clients. Emily was likeable and appeared to really be interested in the position. She was definitely a candidate for a second interview.

Toward the end of our interview, Emily summarized her work experience and discussed how valuable an employee she would be to my organization. I reiterated to Emily what I had written to her about the salary range for the position. She made a face and then blurted out, "I'm not going to work for peanuts!"

I was absolutely stunned! She knew the salary range coming in and if it were not sufficient, why did she accept an interview? Jobs in our field do not always pay well, but I felt that what my organization was offering was reasonable. But we were not going to meet Emily's salary requirement. There was no second interview.

Emily had the right to seek the salary she felt she deserved. But she knew my organization was not offering her pay rate. She wasted time. And to tell an interviewer that her or his organization is paying "peanuts" is just totally inappropriate and insulting interview behavior.

GREAT RESUME! BUT THAT WAS ALL

After combing through so many resumes from individuals who lacked the qualifications and experience for the Vocational Counselor position, I saw Jessica's resume. She had the experience and training. Jessica's resume was awesome!

Jessica was not.

The candidate was scheduled for a 6pm interview. If the interview went well, Jessica could potentially be my next new hire. With her experience, I thought that Jessica could add much to our team.

When the receptionist called and told me that Jessica had arrived, I went to the reception area. My heart sank upon greeting her. Jessica's greeting was lukewarm. She radiated an unpleasant aura. This really took me by surprise.

The interview did not go well. Jessica was slightly rude and her language got a bit rough during the interview, though she used no expletives. She spoke negatively of her colleagues and I got the sense that working with her would be difficult. The interview ended early. Jessica would not be a good fit for us and was sent a rejection letter.

This was not my first time being disappointed in an interview with a candidate who looked good on paper, but it was still shocking to me. Searching for the right candidate can be a tremendous task. So when you think you have found someone who could potentially work out and they interview so poorly, it can be discouraging. You wonder, "How can someone be so accomplished and not present well in an interview?" It does happen, but job seekers should not let this be their experience. Job seekers should strive to present well on paper and in person.

I'M LATE, BUT NO APOLOGY IS NECESSARY

When an interview is scheduled, a candidate is expected to be on time. Arriving 10-15 minutes before your appointment is acceptable. Candidates will be notified if they need to arrive any earlier to complete paperwork. When candidates are running late, and sometimes this happens, contact the interviewer to inform them that you are running late but are still coming to the interview. Apologize to the interviewer both in your message and when you finally arrive for the interview.

Sharon was a candidate for a Senior Vocational Counselor position. She had not arrived at the time of her interview and had not contacted me, so I assumed she would be a no- show. More than 20 minutes later, the receptionist called to tell me that Sharon had arrived for her interview! Just when I had started some other work, she finally showed up. It took me a few minutes to get into interviewer mode.

The interview with Sharon was irritating. She carried on about battling school administrators she felt were getting in the way of her earning an Ivy League degree. Sharon also talked about how she would not have had a child if she could relive her life (TMI. I will talk about that later). I detected an edginess, an obnoxious tone in this candidate that was off-putting, and mind you, this candidate had impressive credentials!

It was quite annoying that at NO time during the interview did Sharon acknowledge or apologize for her tardiness. She acted as if it were perfectly acceptable to get to an interview late. Sharon was a definite "no" for a second interview.

About one month later, Sharon sent me an email saying that she had gotten a very good job. She also decided to throw shade by writing a comment about how some other employer saw her potential and felt she could benefit the community in her new role. Sharon made it seem like not hiring her was my loss. It did not feel like a loss at all! I offered congratulations to her.

Job candidates should not ever respond the way Sharon did to rejection. If you are not hired for a position, be gracious. Thank the interviewer for their time and wish them well in their search. Do not send snarky, snide emails. You will come across as very petty and immature. Years ago, I sent a nice thank you email to an interviewer who had not offered me a position. She sent me a great response, explaining that I was a good candidate, but did not have the skill set she was seeking for the position. The interviewer even gave me suggestions on where to send my resume!

I have received kind thank you emails from candidates who were not hired by me. One candidate even reached out and asked me for some interviewing tips and I offered her my assistance.

When job seeking, it is definitely a good look to be gracious and to be on time for a job interview!

THIS JOB INTERVIEW IS NOT THAT SERIOUS

Candace, a candidate for a Career Coach position, was another person who had a good resume, but a poor interview presentation, like Jessica and Sharon.

This candidate showed no enthusiasm during her interview. Candace barely answered the questions and when asked why she wanted the position, she replied that she needed a job! This was someone who should have known better than to make such a reply. Candace did not seem to take her interview seriously.

A rejection letter was sent to Candace. To my surprise, she emailed me twice and apologized that she did not interview well. Candace attached another copy of her resume and asked for another chance to interview! I sent her a cordial response but I had no intention of considering her for any future opportunities.

RACIST REMARKS ARE NEVER ACCEPTABLE

Donna was a candidate for a Senior Career Specialist position. Throughout the interview, Donna acted a bit more familiar with me than was acceptable. She spoke to me as if we were not friends exactly, but acquaintances, and got a bit too comfortable.

In the middle of answering a question about why she left her last position, Donna made a racist remark. When she saw the look of shock on my face, she tried to walk back her statement. No matter how she tried to clean that one up, she could not. Donna was out of consideration for the position.

Years later, Yolanda, a candidate for a Program Assistant position, was being interviewed by a junior colleague and me. We were having a nice conversation until Yolanda made a racist remark. She laughed as if it were a joke but again, my face registered shock. After the interview, my colleague shook her head in disbelief. Yolanda would not be hired. As with Donna, we did not want to take a chance that she would not treat all of our clients fairly and with the dignity they deserved.

Racist remarks are never acceptable in a job interview. Regrettably, they are all too common in the racially tense environment in which we live today. People do not even have the common sense to keep these comments off their social media accounts. Employers are paying attention, especially when people are alerting companies of their employees' online racist remarks.

DO I HAVE THE JOB?

Liza was a candidate for a Career Counselor position. Her initial interview was conducted over the phone . Candidates should not be too relaxed when interviewing by phone. Treat phone interviews the way you would a face-to-face interview.

Liza did not give good responses to my questions. She came across as being dishonest when it was discovered through our conversation that she did not have the experience she claimed on her resume. Liza was another candidate who talked to me in a familiar way, like we were friends or acquaintances.

My decision was that Liza would not be asked for a second interview. As the interview was wrapping up, Liza laughed and asked "Do I get the job?" I laughed until the realization hit me that she was very serious! Liza was already telling me what her availability was to start the position! My response was that we were still seeing other candidates and would be in touch. Liza was not hired.

About a year later, Liza called me. She had interviewed for a position in another division in my organization. Liza wanted to know if I had heard anything about her candidacy! She really had some boundary issues! I had no knowledge about hiring decisions made by other divisions and would not tell her anything if I did know! Liza was a very poor job candidate. She was dishonest on her resume and demonstrated inappropriate behavior.

STOP WHINING

Job seekers are cautioned time and again to not focus on the negative aspects of their previous jobs on an interview. Of course, not everything in a job is perfect. But focusing upon all that was wrong instead of what went well and what you contributed to a position will turn a prospective employer off.

In my interviews, some candidates freely complained about poor relationships with supervisors and what they felt were unfair or unreasonable program policies. Believe me I get it, having dealt with these issues in my own work life. But in my own job interviews, the good work that I did for previous organizations was emphasized, not the difficulties. Job candidates are encouraged to do the same when interviewing. Employers are interested in the work that you have done and what you can bring to their organization. Complaining about undesirable situations in a past job does not make for a good impression in an interview.

Eric was interviewed for a position as an Outreach Coordinator. His whining on the first interview cost him a second interview. The initial interview was going well at first. Then Eric was asked about the kind of supervisor he liked working with and that is when the interview fizzled. Eric went on a rant about past supervisors and how he did not like to be micromanaged. Eric made it sound like he was resistant to supervision because of past work experiences. When the interview ended, Eric's name was placed on my rejection list. I would have been Eric's supervisor had he been hired and was not going to deal with his attitude.

There are undesirable situations in every job. Again, the important thing during an interview is to sell yourself and what you can contribute to a job, not harp on the negative and whine about past jobs.

TOO MUCH INFORMATION (TMI)

When a job seeker goes on a job interview, their focus should be on promoting their experience, skills and expressing sincere interest in the position for which they have applied. But they should not share TMI (too much information), especially personal and sensitive information, on an interview.

Leah was being interviewed for a Vocational Counselor position. She was pleasant and well-spoken, but it turned out that her experience, as she described it, was not sufficient for the position.

Just as we were wrapping up, Leah told me that she was facing eviction. Taken aback, I responded "I'm sorry to hear that." For me, that was TMI. Not that I am coldhearted, but it is so uncomfortable to hear about a candidate's personal problems during a job interview.

Career articles on the topic of sharing personal information during a job interview suggest that job seekers need to avoid sharing TMI on a job interview. If asked by the interviewer, a candidate can talk about things like hobbies, travel, books. Employers do not need to know about a candidate's bar hopping or socializing habits. Job seekers should keep their private business private and monitor their social media accounts that employers may see.

There were other interviews with candidates in which they shared personal information. It was always uncomfortable for me. The best that I could do was acknowledge the candidate's statement and bring the focus back to the interview.

SHE'S WEARING JEANS

Are jeans acceptable to wear to an interview? Most career experts say definitely not, while others say it really depends on the company at which you are interviewing. Throughout my years of interviewing and hiring, the answer has been a firm "no" at my organizations.

I rarely encounter candidates who come to interviews inappropriately dressed. It happened once and really surprised me. The Office Manager had given me the heads up about Amy's attire. She was wearing jeans. The candidate was pleasant, but one of the things that concerned me more than the jeans was that the candidate seemed a bit casual in her attitude. The position she was interviewing for, Program Assistant, required someone who was very professional in manner. This person would have heavy customer contact. After speaking with Amy, I determined that she would not be a good fit for the position.

When interviewing candidates, my focus is more on their experience, skills, and attitude. If a good candidate came to an interview in jeans or other inappropriate attire, I would probably ask them, tactfully, to wear different attire during a second interview.

A woman recently told the true story of a job candidate who had recently been released from prison. She went on a job interview dressed in pajama bottoms! People at the company were laughing at her. It turned out that no one had ever taught her how to dress for an interview. The employer who interviewed her saw something in this candidate and hired her! The employer mentored this woman and she turned out to be a stellar employee. Kudos to this employer! No doubt she changed this woman's life in a great way.

When I interview candidates, it is perfectly acceptable for them to be dressed in business casual attire. Some career specialists even recommend that a candidate dress one level above the position for which they have applied. Some examples for interview clothing for men include dress slacks or khakis, a shirt with a collar (tie optional), socks and dress shoes. A woman can wear dress slacks, a skirt (not too short), blouse, sweater, jacket (optional) and closed toe shoes with hosiery (although hosiery seems to be quite optional these days). No jeans, tight or revealing clothing, sneakers, sandals or flip flops. There are tons of articles in books and online career sites about appropriate interview clothing.

THE NO- SHOW CANDIDATES

Reviewing resumes after you have posted a job announcement is a demanding task. Employers can get flooded with resumes. At times I had to review several resumes before finding one resume of a qualified candidate who could be contacted for an interview.

When an interviewer has contacted a job seeker and set up an interview that they agreed to, it is really unprofessional and the height of bad manners to not show up. Not showing up and offering no explanatory call or email is not acceptable.

In the past few years, this no-show incident has happened to me at least six times, twice in the month of September 2017! Two of the candidates even called or emailed me to confirm their appointments, and then still failed to show up! Interviewing is time consuming and if the candidates were not going to keep the interview appointment they should have informed me.

There is no problem with changing one's mind about an employment opportunity. Whenever I changed my mind about an interview, the employer was always informed. This gave them the opportunity to free up their schedule for another candidate. Calling or sending an email cancelling an interview is much appreciated and the professional thing to do when a job seeker is no longer interested in a position. Busy employers do not have time to waste. Busy job seekers do not have time to waste.

PART THREE:
MY PERSONAL EXPERIENCES WITH UNPROFESSIONAL INTERVIEWERS

My experience as a job seeker has been good most times. Even if I ultimately was not offered a particular position, it was good to have had the interview experience. One can still learn from unsuccessful interviews and I learned from mine.

There have been some difficult interview experiences in my career. Most of the time, it was the interviewer who was unsatisfactory. These difficult interview experiences taught me that not all interviewers are professional, and that it was important to maintain my professionalism at all times when interviewing.

The first scenario in this section recounts an incident in which my interview behavior was unprofessional. It was a true teaching moment and it never happened again!

DUCKING OUT

It was summertime. I was a college student looking for a temporary job. My interview was for a position with the New York City Summer Youth Employment Program as a Senior Counselor.

My interviewer, a young man named Mr. Baines, was totally unprofessional. While interviewing me, Mr. Baines was on the phone and shuffled papers. His behavior was rude. An interview is not a time to be multitasking. Mr. Baines also had a bad attitude and spoke gruffly to me. It was a puzzling and infuriating experience. To me, this was no serious interview.

Someone called during the interview and Mr. Baines had to step out of the room. I was upset and decided to step out of the room as well and go home! I had never done that on an interview and was surprised at myself. Mr. Baines must have been puzzled when he returned to the office to find me gone! He behaved so poorly he probably did not care. There was one less candidate for him to worry about.

My action was inexcusable. What I should have done was continue the interview and make a graceful exit at the end. By ducking out of the interview, my candidacy ended. Who knows how many people Mr. Baines told about what I had done? That episode was definitely not one of my finest moments as a job seeker and it never happened again.

THE INTERROGATION

One of the hardest topics for a job seeker to tackle in an interview is the subject of termination from employment. It can be overwhelming and disheartening to discuss a termination.

I was once terminated from a position and after getting over the difficult emotions, started my job search. Within a week of sending out a couple of resumes, an employer called me for an interview for a Career Manager position. There was much preparation on my part for the interview. When asked about my termination, it would be addressed head on with no negativity on my part.

During the interview, my attitude was positive, but the interviewer's was negative, and his attitude ruined the interview.

Mr. Perez, the interviewer, was sternly questioning me about the termination. It was quite unsettling, even more so because he had an assistant sitting in during the interview. Mr. Perez asked questions about the termination for nearly ten minutes, almost sounding confrontational! I was thinking "I have answered the question. Let us move on now. Focus on my experience, education and skills." Surprisingly, Mr. Perez told me at the end of the interview that he would like for me to come back for a second interview! I thanked him.

I had good experience and skills and wanted to be judged by those, not by one error in judgment on my part. People make mistakes. I was better than this and was not going to put myself in a position to be browbeaten by this man or someone else at his organization.

Mr. Perez received an email from me thanking him for the interview and declining his second interview. He responded, seeking an explanation. I wrote briefly about exploring other employment opportunities. Eventually a position opened for me. My new employer was interested in my experience and skills, not fixated on a mistake.

When interviewing people who have been terminated from a position, I never want them to feel beaten down by me. Having been terminated from a job beats you down enough. In an interview, we discuss the termination briefly, the candidate tells me what they have learned from the experience, and then we move on. There are people who were terminated from jobs who went on to do really good work. Author J.K. Rowling is a shining example!

WHAT WAS THAT ABOUT?

I was interviewing for a position as a Senior Career Counselor at a local college and it was pretty intense. My first interview was conducted by a committee of at least seven people sitting around a table asking me questions. Having had that type of interview experience at a previous time, it was not as daunting as it could have been, but I was certainly kept on my toes!

The first interview went well. An invitation was extended to me for a second interview with three of the executive administrators at the college--Ms. Danes, Ms. Jordan and Ms. Iannotti. Initially, they made me feel very comfortable as we talked.

The conversation was progressing nicely. I answered their questions and tried not to ramble on. The interview turned a bit sour when I was making a reference to a report. Suddenly Ms. Jordan cut me off, saying "we know what the report says!" in a snappish tone. What was *that* about? It was important for me to demonstrate my knowledge of the current literature in the field. Without missing a beat, Ms. Iannotti jumped right in and asked me another question. Ms. Jordan's rudeness shocked but did not disable me. Our conversation continued, but Ms. Jordan did not ask me any more questions. The interview soon ended. A few weeks later, they hired me for the position.

TAKING HER SWEET TIME

I showed up for my interview for a Vocational Coordinator position a few minutes early, as is my practice. You never want to take a chance with the unreliable New York City subway system! I introduced myself to the receptionist and told her about my appointment with Ms. Grace. She had me sit in the waiting area.

Time passed. I was still seated 30 minutes later and there was no sign of Ms. Grace! I thought, "Today IS my appointment, right?" Even the receptionist was looking at me with a puzzled expression. She tried calling Ms. Grace.

Forty minutes after my scheduled interview, Ms. Grace showed up! My head was exploding!

Ms. Grace did not even apologize for being late! She definitely got off on the wrong foot with me. Interviewers need to be as mindful of candidates' time as we are of theirs. When an interviewer calls someone in for an interview, she or he should be there to greet the candidate, not saunter into the office over 40 minutes after you were supposed to meet! I can still remember how Ms. Grace walked in, casually waving her briefcase. Instead of acknowledging me, Ms. Grace went directly up to her office.

The interview was far from memorable. A few weeks later, Ms. Grace offered me the position. I accepted, but did not stay with the organization long. Ms. Grace's rude and inconsiderate behavior continued throughout my time there. My work was very good in spite of her. Our first encounter during that initial interview should have been a clue to me that my employment experience at her agency would not be a positive one.

PART FOUR:
MAKING DISAPPOINTING HIRES

Though most of the candidates hired by me work out well, I have had my share of disappointing hires. Candidates are appraised to the best of my ability, but bad hiring decisions are still made on occasion. Sometimes job seekers pretend to be a certain kind of candidate that they are not. Integrity matters in the job search and on the job! A job seeker, once hired, cannot expect to get so comfortable in a position that they behave anyway they choose without consequences.

JEFFREY

Hiring Jeffrey was a disastrous decision!

The process started when an initial interview was conducted over the phone with Jeffrey, a candidate for an Outreach Coordinator position. During the interview, Jeffrey was articulate, enthusiastic, and you could feel his energy through the phone! He emphasized his interpersonal and collaborative skills. Jeffrey's interview was one of the best, and he was offered a second interview. Jeffrey was very interested in the position.

When Jeffrey came in for his second interview, he was initially quiet and reserved. But Jeffrey did well in the second interview, where he was asked to do a brief presentation for some colleagues and me. He was very impressive. After a final interview with my supervisor, Jeffrey was hired.

Jeffrey's first three weeks in the position were good, but then things suddenly and inexplicably deteriorated. He left the organization shortly before his probationary period ended. It was my intention to let him go and perhaps he sensed his termination coming.

It was baffling to me that Jeffrey had problems following my directives. For example, one day Jeffrey emailed me a few minutes before he was due in the office to tell me he would not be in. When he reported for work the next day, we spoke about the organization's policy for calling out sick. He was supposed to contact me at least a couple of hours before he was due for work. A few weeks later, Jeffrey again failed to follow the policy for calling out sick and was given a written reprimand.

Jeffrey also alienated other staff by acting like he was smarter than they were and making snarky comments. Not surprisingly, they disliked him and criticized his work. He received regular supervision and support from me. But Jeffrey did not want to hear about where his work needed improvement. It really frustrated me. He would not accept any accountability. Once, he attended an important community meeting and neglected to bring any outreach materials with him! He was the Outreach Coordinator! My supervisor attended the meeting, arriving ahead of him, and was so embarrassed when Jeffrey showed up empty handed. After confronting him the next day, it was my decision that Jeffrey had to be removed from the position.

In the end, Jeffrey did not have the maturity for the position. He wanted to do things his way and not take instruction. Jeffrey was probably not used to supervision, though he claimed otherwise in his interview. My organization was not the right setting for him.

ESME

Esme was hired as a Career Services Manager. She presented well in the interview, displayed maturity, had a sincere interest in the position, and possessed good skills and experience as a manager. During the interview, Esme emphasized the importance of professional workplace behavior.

Initially, Esme did well in her job. She had the ability to quickly learn her job and get things done. Esme worked well with the clients and her colleagues. She was responsible for supervising some staff as well.

Esme was expected to help run our department, but she seemed to be disinterested. She waited for me to give directives and was reluctant to offer suggestions and input into our programming. That was confusing to me because being a leader was her job!

After a year, the situation with Esme became concerning. Her staff complained that Esme showed no leadership and they left the organization. Some of the clients even complained about her, saying that she acted like she was superior to them and did not care about their program needs. I documented incidents where Esme did not follow through on work assignments and compiled client complaints about her work.

One incident that was particularly irksome occurred was when I was out sick for nearly two weeks with the flu. When I returned to the office, I discovered that Esme had allowed calls on our client hotline to pile up in my absence! Nearly 50 phone calls from potential clients went unanswered until my return. Who ignores individuals who express interest in their organization's services? This was another example of the indifference Esme was displaying toward her job.

I spoke frankly to Esme about my concerns and those brought up by others. Esme seemed to think everyone else was at fault for her bad attitude and poor work! In spite of the documentation presented, she acknowledged no fault.

This was not what I expected from Esme when she was hired. Instead of being a partner in our work, she had become a drain on our department. Her behavior had taken a 180 degree turn and she offered no explanation. There was little of the professionalism Esme had so emphasized in her interviews. Esme was let go from her position.

What kind of employee do job seekers claim to be when they interview for a position? If they claim that they are always punctual, work well with others, are organized, etc. they must be sure this is what their employer sees after they hire them. If they have an issue that interferes with their work, they should get help. Employees should not give their employer reason to become dissatisfied with their work and let them go.

PART FIVE:
A SPECIAL NOTE OF CAUTION

This section highlights a series of emails that my staff and I received from a disgruntled candidate, Adrian, who was not accepted into one of my organization's training programs. His interviews (we saw him twice) were not good and he was seen as a potentially problematic candidate. We were right in our judgment and decision.

After reading the emails, you will obviously see why we rejected Adrian. My point in sharing this is to show that this is NOT the way a serious candidate behaves when they receive news of a rejection. As a result of Adrian's tirade, we banned him from our facility and from applying for any of our programs in the future. Reading these emails made me wonder if he would take the same course of action with an employer who rejected him.

Adrian's rant started when he received an email informing him that he had not been accepted into one of our training programs. These are his responses (as he wrote them, except for the expletives, which I decided to edit):

"That's rude, u people probably don't help people anyway and somebody gave u a chance, shame on u and the slaves working there. Lol clowns."

We were stunned! We ignored this message, but Adrian kept writing us:

"Like I said f--- yall. Im glad my wife and home is better than yours , cause I would feel a certain way. And take that weave out u look fake, and that fat ugly b---- (he directed this at me) that shook my hand and help u with the decision looks miserable, u dummies clear up my schedule so I can do better s---. You don't like these emails don't respond back cause I can keep them coming. And I might come up there to shred my info."

Again, we did not respond to his email, but the entire staff was alerted by me that Adrian was sending inappropriate emails and that the police should be called if he entered the premises.

Two days later, Adrian was at it again! Mind you, we never once responded to his messages.

"Like I said your free to come over so you can see how I live, stop shopping at payless, and by the way I am more than qualified to do your job. How did you start by serving coffee or shining shoes? And I am sure u came from a program you look recycled and used! You b------ lost a great candidate I am stronger, smarter and better looking than all you trannies, that's what I thought you were a TRANNIE…..LOL and p.s. my shoes cost more than your whole Rainbow wardrobe. Well im about to watch my 55 inch with my attractive b---- I bet whomever u messing with cant say that…ahahahahahaha."

Still no response on our part. A few weeks later, Adrian sent one more message to another staff member, blaming her for his failure to be accepted into the program:

"It's amazing that u had neither the decency or b---- to tell me why I wasn't selected. You caused the initial confusion when u misinformed me and others about needing a driver's license. I had to let your coworkers know how much I loathed them. I will make it a point to let u guys know my level of success when I achieve it! Again u practically begged people to come back I did not once but three times…u suck."

I showed these emails to the youth at my workshop to make the point about how job seekers should not handle rejection and the importance of monitoring their digital footprint. They could not believe what they were reading! Yes, this is extreme. Who would want to work around someone like Adrian? Good interviewers try hard to screen out people like him. Adrian actually wanted to enter a training that required very good people and customer service skills! Unbelievable!   Adrian needed an anger management program.

We certainly made the right decision by rejecting his application.   Adrian's poor behavior and attitude ruined his interviews and cost him an opportunity for possible success.

PART SIX:
MY FEEL-GOOD INTERVIEWS

Every interviewer and job seeker should have an occasional feel-good interviewing experience! Interviewing is stressful. How wonderful it is to have an experience that is not only pleasurable, but results in a good outcome as well.

In this section, you will read about three of my feel-good interviews. The first anecdote recalls one of my best job interviews, which resulted in a nice surprise for me. Two anecdotes follow about the best interviews I have ever conducted in my career. One candidate eventually worked with me. The other candidate impressed me at a screening interview.

THE METHADONE CLINIC

Years ago I interviewed for a position as a Vocational Counselor for a drug treatment program at a local hospital. Two staff members, Charles and Maria, interviewed me. Charles took the lead in the interview. Maria was sitting in the background, but she asked me questions as well. They were very good interviewers, personable and focused on their task. Surprisingly, there was nothing stressful about the interview. It had gone well and I was offered a second interview.

I thought hard about the interview and the position. My decision was to decline the second interview and pursue other employment opportunities.

A human resources staff member from the hospital called regarding a second interview. I thanked her but declined. She surprised me when she went on to tell me that Charles and Maria were interested in hiring me for a better position than the one for which they had interviewed me! She had my attention!

I reported for the second interview and eventually, was offered the position as the Senior Vocational Counselor at a methadone drug treatment clinic. Maria was my immediate supervisor (hooray)! The only thing I knew about methadone was what my late friend Rico told me about it. It was controversial. There was a stigma attached to people using it. Critics said that people using methadone were not really trying to quit drugs, were not serious about recovery, and that the methadone was just another drug.

The methadone patients were special to me and I loved my work with them all. It was my responsibility to provide vocational rehabilitation services to any of the more than 400 patients who wanted assistance with finding employment or pursuing further education or training. Going to work was enjoyable.

One of my strongest memories of my job at the methadone clinic was a counseling session with a patient named Rosemary. She was a mature woman with one of the most pleasant personalities.

Rosemary decided that she wanted to look for a job. After all of the job preparation activity, she was actively out looking for employment.

One afternoon, Rosemary came to see me to talk about an interview she had gone on. She did not get the job. Rosemary was upset because she really wanted that job. She cried for about five minutes. Seeing her in pain hurt me. Rosemary and I knew that she had something to contribute somewhere, so we continued working together. Everyone wants to do something meaningful with their lives.

When I left the position, the patients surprised me and gave me a beautiful plaque that is on display in my living room. To this day, these patients are still in my thoughts.

This employment experience shows that job seekers have to take the interviewing process seriously. One never knows what the end result will be. My interview for one position led to me being offered a better position. In addition to that, Maria, who was one of my best supervisors, stays in touch with me and has helped opened up other doors for me throughout my career.

MARY

Mary is a sterling example of a successful job candidate.

She initially interviewed for a position as a Program Assistant. Mary had come from a corporate background and did not have much work experience in nonprofit settings. Mary held an Associate's Degree and was in her last semester of a Bachelor's degree program in Human Services.

There was something compelling about Mary's presentation, her confidence, and her ebullience. Mary had an energy about her that was sorely needed in our department. The more we talked, the more I wanted to hire Mary! Other candidates had been interviewed, but she was the frontrunner for the position.

Mary was recommended to my supervisor for a second interview. My supervisor, a tough interviewer, liked her as well. We hired Mary and she did not disappoint.

From day one, Mary was on the move. She wanted to know everything about her job, the department, and the organization. Mary worked very hard. She took on different tasks and made sure that all of them were done properly. Mary answered the phones, returned phone messages, sent out letters, maintained files, greeted customers, covered the front desk when needed, and performed other duties.

Mary started her new job around flu season and was so upset when she got sick and missed a couple of days of work. Mary was so apologetic when she called and left messages to notify me that she would not be in due to illness. She was so afraid of jeopardizing her job, but Mary was assured that she was not going to lose her job for becoming ill.

I really appreciated the way Mary involved herself in the department's programming. She sat in on training classes to learn more about our programs. The customers were accustomed to seeing Mary in the classes and enthusiastically greeted her in the mornings. Some would go to Mary for assistance.

After observing one of our training classes, Mary came to my office. She was so effusive! Mary talked about how proud she was to work for an organization that offered the training we did, and how great it was to see the customers learning in our classes. It was wonderful to see and hear that Mary was enjoying her work.

After a few months on the job, I noticed something about my new employee Mary. She was not a Program Assistant. Mary was a Career Coach! The Career Coaches provided guidance and support to the customers and graduates of our training programs. Mary was effectively performing her duties as a Program Assistant, but I felt that she was meant to work full-time with the customers. Mary loved the classes we offered and enjoyed working with the customers. And the customers felt very comfortable interacting with her. Mary had the most important qualities necessary to be an effective Career Coach--passion about the work and great customer service skills.

There was a conversation with my supervisor about promoting Mary. She was not in the Program Assistant position long, but my feelings about this move were strong and positive. My supervisor asked me to review Mary's school grades and discuss the position with her. Mary's grades were pretty good. When I spoke to Mary about becoming a Career Coach, she was thrilled, but she was concerned about her ability to do the job. She was assured that she would get the training and support she needed. In fact, we gave her a two-month tryout in the role before she made a decision about taking the position. At the end of the tryout, Mary agreed to accept the position of Career Coach.

I had never had that happen before in my career. But Mary was such a standout employee, and she needed to be in the position that fit her best. It was important to me that Mary be satisfied in her new work and she was! It certainly did not hurt that she made more money! She helped our team immeasurably. Mary will always be a feel-good hire for me!

CALVIN: A MOST MEMORABLE INTERVIEW

I was working as a Senior Career Advisor at a local workforce center. We often had on-site job recruitment events. It was my responsibility to interview job candidates and then recommend them (or not) to the employer for an immediate follow up interview. We saw customers randomly, so I never knew who would end up at my desk.

One job seeker who came to our event was Calvin, a young Black male around 18 or 19 years old. He was neatly dressed in a white shirt, tie and slacks, and he was quite personable. Calvin's paperwork was neat and thorough. He explained to me that he came to the recruitment event because he really wanted a job. Calvin disclosed to me that he had committed a crime, was held accountable by the juvenile justice system, and now wanted to work. Calvin reported that he had entered a youth program that gave him job readiness preparation and in fact, had come to the event with others from his program.

Calvin reminded me of a character from a movie scene I saw years ago in which a young Black man was being interviewed for a position. Once he revealed that he had committed a crime in the past, the employer shut down. My interviewee Calvin did not have to worry about me doing the same. We had a great interview and his honesty was appreciated. Calvin displayed a maturity that some adults interviewed by me sorely lacked. I told him that he was approved for a second interview with the employer! He was directed to the next area where he would continue with the hiring process. It bothers me that I did not follow up on Calvin, because he left such an impression upon me. It is partly because of my encounter with him that I went on to provide employment services to formerly incarcerated individuals, to work with other Calvins.

Calvin was a great example of what a young person transitioning out of the juvenile justice system can accomplish with the right support and positive behaviors and attitudes. What a memorable, feel-good interview!

CONCLUSION

"What Were They Thinking? Avoid Behaviors and Attitudes That Can Ruin A Job Interview" was written to help job seekers, especially new job seekers, avoid the behavioral and attitudinal missteps that can hurt a job interview. This book offers important lessons about the job seeker's need to be mindful of negative behaviors and attitudes that can motivate an employer to rule them out for a position.

Hard job skills matter, but behaviors and attitudes matter too, in some cases, more than your skills! There may currently be a great deal of incivility and hostility in peoples' behaviors and attitudes, but professionalism, civility, and good communication never go out of style with employers.

Part One of this book, featuring a blog post written by me a few years ago, outlined some brief job seeking tips. These included having a professional email and voicemail message; bringing extra copies of a resume with you to an interview or screening event; showing up for your interview; and using appropriate language. The book discussed the elements of a good interview. Hopefully, job seekers also have a better grasp of how to answer the question about their professional areas that need development, also referred to as weaknesses. And job seekers should remember to send a thank you note after every interview. That should be a standard practice.

The real-life accounts of my experiences with job candidates who derailed their interviews because of poor behaviors and attitudes were the focus of Part Two. You met candidates such as Eldon, who repeatedly questioned me about his being "thrown into the job" and was then impatient with the organization's hiring process; Emily, who openly scoffed at the salary being offered; Jessica, the candidate with the great resume and poor attitude; Sharon, the tardy candidate who failed to acknowledge her lateness and then threw shade via email when she was hired elsewhere; and Candace, an indifferent candidate who failed to take her interview seriously. She then had the audacity to ask for another interview when she received her rejection letter!

Other unsuccessful candidates from Part Two include Donna and Yolanda, who made racist remarks during their interviews; Liza, the candidate with boundary issues, who embellished her resume and interviewed poorly; Eric, the candidate ruled out when he openly complained about past supervisors; Leah, who shared too much personal information (TMI) about a pending eviction; and Amy, the candidate inappropriately dressed for her interview. There was also a brief discussion about interview candidates who were no-shows for their interviews and failed to cancel their appointments.

Part Three looked at my job interview experiences with unprofessional interviewers. Let me re-emphasize--my behavior in my interview with Mr. Baines was inappropriate. Mr. Baines was unprofessional but that was no excuse for me to leave the interview. I could have completed the interview, thanked Mr. Baines and gone on my way. Had he offered me the position, it would have been my responsibility to weigh my decision carefully.

The other interviewers described in Part Three were either late and unapologetic for their interview with me (Ms. Grace); very demeaning and browbeating (Mr. Perez); or rude and snappish (Ms. Jordan). Each incident was unsettling, but in two cases, the employers still offered me the positions and in one other, the employer offered me a second interview. These experiences taught me that interviewers are not always professional in their behaviors and attitudes, but candidates should maintain professionalism in spite of the interviewer's presentation. I also learned what to avoid doing when interviewing job candidates. My practice as an interviewer is to be punctual, courteous and attentive to every candidate. A candidate is not browbeaten by me because of any mistakes they have made.

Jeffrey and Esme in Part Four were two employees who diminished the quality of my team with their unprofessionalism, though both had emphasized the importance of professionalism in their interviews with me. In their positions, they failed to work up to or maintain the standard that was expected, in spite of the support and opportunities given for professional growth. Jeffrey was gone from his position before his probation period ended. Esme was eventually discharged from her position. Integrity matters in your job search and when you are employed.

Who will forget Adrian in Part Five? We interviewed this candidate twice and honestly did not believe him to be a good fit for our program. Adrian's nasty, outrageous and abusive emails reinforced our decision. One of my concerns was that he would come to our office for a confrontation, but thankfully that did not occur. Adrian was banned from our office and would not receive any future consideration for our programs. Anyone who has to work or live around this abusive man is very unfortunate. No one should ever respond to rejection in the manner in which Adrian responded to us.

Remembering one of my great personal interviews and discussing the interviews of Mary and Calvin helped me end the book on a feel-good note in Part Six. Hiring Mary was truly one of the bright moments in my career. Every organization needs a Mary (or two, or three)! Meeting Calvin, the young man who had recently left the juvenile justice system and came to our recruitment event to find employment and change his life, was inspiring. I went on to provide career services to formerly incarcerated individuals because of my experience with Calvin.

A job interview is not the time for arrogance, coarseness, lateness, whining, racist comments, not showing up and not calling to cancel or reschedule an interview if necessary, displaying poor boundaries, deception, joking around, and disclosing too much information (TMI). Self-defeating behaviors and attitudes can hurt a job seeker's chances of being hired for a position and considered for future opportunities. The good news is that job seekers can avoid displaying these behaviors and attitudes with proper interview preparation.

I marveled at a video clip of CNBC's program "The Job Interview" in which a young lady interviewed for a customer service position with a pet company. This candidate definitely needed more interview preparation.

She showed little energy and enthusiasm. Additionally, she was VERY negative about working with other people, calling that the "downside" of a job! She further stated "I find more comfort with animals than I do with humans."Her interviewers definitely had their "What was she thinking?" moment with this candidate. This candidate came across as being unwilling to work cooperatively with others. She had the wrong attitude for this customer service position. I really hope she received the feedback she needed to become a better interviewer and a better employee.

Preparing for a job interview is crucial so that during an interview, candidates can focus on the business of demonstrating that they are the best candidate for a job. Job seekers need to do more than have a good resume and appropriate interview attire. They should be mindful of their behaviors and attitudes. A job interview is the time to be punctual, energetic, attentive, positive, engaging, expressing sincere interest in the position, and exuding professionalism.

Job seekers should closely examine their behaviors and attitudes. They can resolve to address any defeatist attitudes and behaviors that can hurt a job search (and one's career). Talking to a professional career coach or trusted associates can be helpful. Taking advantage of the career resources discussed in the next section can help make job seekers more competitive candidates who are well prepared for future interviews and employment opportunities.

A job seeker can be exceptional! They can be a feel-good candidate! Remember Mary and Calvin.

A FEW HELPFUL
RESOURCES

The following is a brief list of resources that I have found to be helpful for individuals engaged in a job search, especially new job seekers. These resources have also been useful to me personally in further developing my career and counseling job seeking clients.

As discussed in this publication, soft skills such as punctuality, problem solving, time management, conflict resolution, decision making and others are crucial to career success. For more information about soft skills and why they matter to employers, visit the National Soft Skills Association website at *www.nationalsoftskills.org*

Need a list of questions you may be asked in a job interview? Want suggestions on what to wear for a job interview? Ready to send a well written thank you note after an interview? Wondering how to avoid sharing too much information (TMI) on an interview? Unsure of how to address salary requirements with a potential interviewer? Feeling nervous about how to respond to an illegal interview question? Preparing for an interview by phone or Skype? These and other career related topics can be found on numerous online career sites. Sites like LinkedIn *(www.linkedin.com)*; Monster*(www.monster.com)*; Idealist Careers *(www.idealistcareers.org)*; CareerBuilder *(www.careerbuilder.com)*; Indeed *(www.indeed.com)*; Glassdoor *(www.glassdoor.com); and* The Muse *(www.themuse.com)* feature informative articles. Career specialists also post on Facebook, Instagram and Twitter and other social media sites.

Smart Brief *(www.smartbrief.com)*bills itself as the "leading digital media publication of targeted business news and industry information." Smart Brief publishes e-newsletters in industries including Business, Education, Finance, Food & Beverage, Health

Care, Retail, Tech, Marketing & Advertising, Life Sciences and Technology, Infrastructure, Energy and Chemicals, Aviation & Aerospace, Travel and Hospitality and others. The publications "Smart Brief on Your Career" and "Smart Brief on Workforce" regularly feature articles on job interviewing strategies and achieving success in the workplace. Past article titles on interviewing include "Give Better Answers to Tough Interview Questions" and "Why Interviewers Ask About Your Strengths and Weaknesses."

Subscriptions to Smart Brief e-newsletters are free. Sign up for them at www.smartbrief.com I have subscriptions to some of the Smart Brief e-newsletters and read them daily. They are highly informative and keep me abreast of pressing issues facing employees and employers in various industries.

Job seekers residing in or near New York City definitely want to visit the New York Public Library's premiere business library, the Science, Industry, and Business Library (SIBL). Located at 188 Madison Avenue in Manhattan, SIBL's Job Search Central is a tremendous resource. SIBL offers online career exploration and job searching tools, and services from pro bono Career Coaches who can meet with job seekers.

SIBL also offers a wealth of ongoing career workshops. Topics include how to use SIBL's career resources, resume writing, interviewing, setting up a LinkedIn account for the job search, networking, starting your career, making career transitions, and others. SIBL's website is *https://www.nypl.org/locations/sibl*

Lynda.com's mission is "to help you learn the skills you need to achieve your full potential." Lynda.com, a part of LinkedIn, is a global online learning platform offering a video library of hundreds of courses taught by industry experts. Courses are available in a range of fields including Business, Design, Software Development, Web Development, Photography and more.

Lynda.com has useful courses on interviewing including "Acing Your Interview." There is also a "Learning Path" series of courses on soft skills titled "Master In- Demand Professional Soft Skills." The courses in this series help job seekers gain essential skills in communication, critical thinking and being a team player.

Some course titles include "Teamwork Foundations," "Critical Thinking," and "Effective Listening."

Basic and Premium Membership Plans are offered by Lynda.com and potential members can take advantage of Lynda.com's 30-day free trial. Individuals who hold a New York Public Library card can access Lynda.com's courses through the library's account. Visit Lynda.com's website at *www.lynda.com*

Job seekers who have attended college should include visits to their college's Career Services Office in their job search plan. A wealth of services are available to current students and alumni. College career services include internship placement, job search assistance, workshops, resume writing, mock interviewing, career counseling, onsite recruitment events, and more.

Finally, local public libraries and career centers around the country offer free services for job seekers including resume writing, interview preparation, and on-site employer recruitment events. To locate a local career center, a job seeker can visit the US Department of Labor, Employment and Training Administration's CareerOneStop website (www.careeronestop.org) or call 1-877-872-5627 (1-877-US2-JOBS) or TTY 1-877-889-5627.